The **FIXER'S** Guide to...
PULLEYS

Written by **JOHN WOOD**

Illustrated by **AMY LI**

BookLife
PUBLISHING

©2020
BookLife Publishing Ltd.
King's Lynn
Norfolk PE30 4LS

ISBN: 978-1-83927-069-7

Written by:
John Wood

Edited by:
Madeline Tyler

Illustrated by:
Amy Li

Designed by:
Drue Rintoul

A catalogue record for this book is available from the British Library.

All rights reserved. Printed in Malaysia.

All facts, statistics, web addresses and URLs in this book were verified as valid and accurate at time of writing. No responsibility for any changes to external websites or references can be accepted by either the author or publisher.

Photo Credits

All images courtesy of Shutterstock.com. With thanks to Getty Images, Thinkstock Photo and iStockphoto.

Recurring images (cover and internals) – Guliveris (background pattern), Agor2012, robuart (cogs), Steve Paint (arrows). Cover – MG Drachal, Tarikdiz. 4–5 – Akifune. 6–7 – Ron Zmiri, South O Boy. 8–9 – bogdanhoda, Heide Pinkall, Nielskliim, lunamarina, New Africa, COLOMBO NICOLA, Spiroview Inc. 10–11 – SKatzenberger, Gorvik, Paul Vinten. 12–13 – ndoeljindoel, pathdoc. 14–15 – OldskoolDesign, Madam Kaye. 16–17 – Benjamin Clapp, Kim Christensen, deela dee.

CONTENTS

PAGE 4   Meet the Fixer
PAGE 6   Pulleys
PAGE 10   Parts of a Pulley
PAGE 12   How a Pulley Works
PAGE 14   Fixed or Free?
PAGE 16   More Wheels, More Power
PAGE 18   Let's Build a Toy Lift
PAGE 24   Glossary and Index

Words that look like this can be found in the glossary on page 24.

MEET THE FIXER

Oh no! Sorry — the Fixer has just eaten breakfast. He is a very messy eater. Say sorry, Fixer.

Pfflblululupgh.

Believe it or not, the Fixer is the smartest being in the universe when it comes to machines.

A machine is an object that makes a job easier to do. The Fixer wants to teach you about one of the simplest types of machine: a pulley.

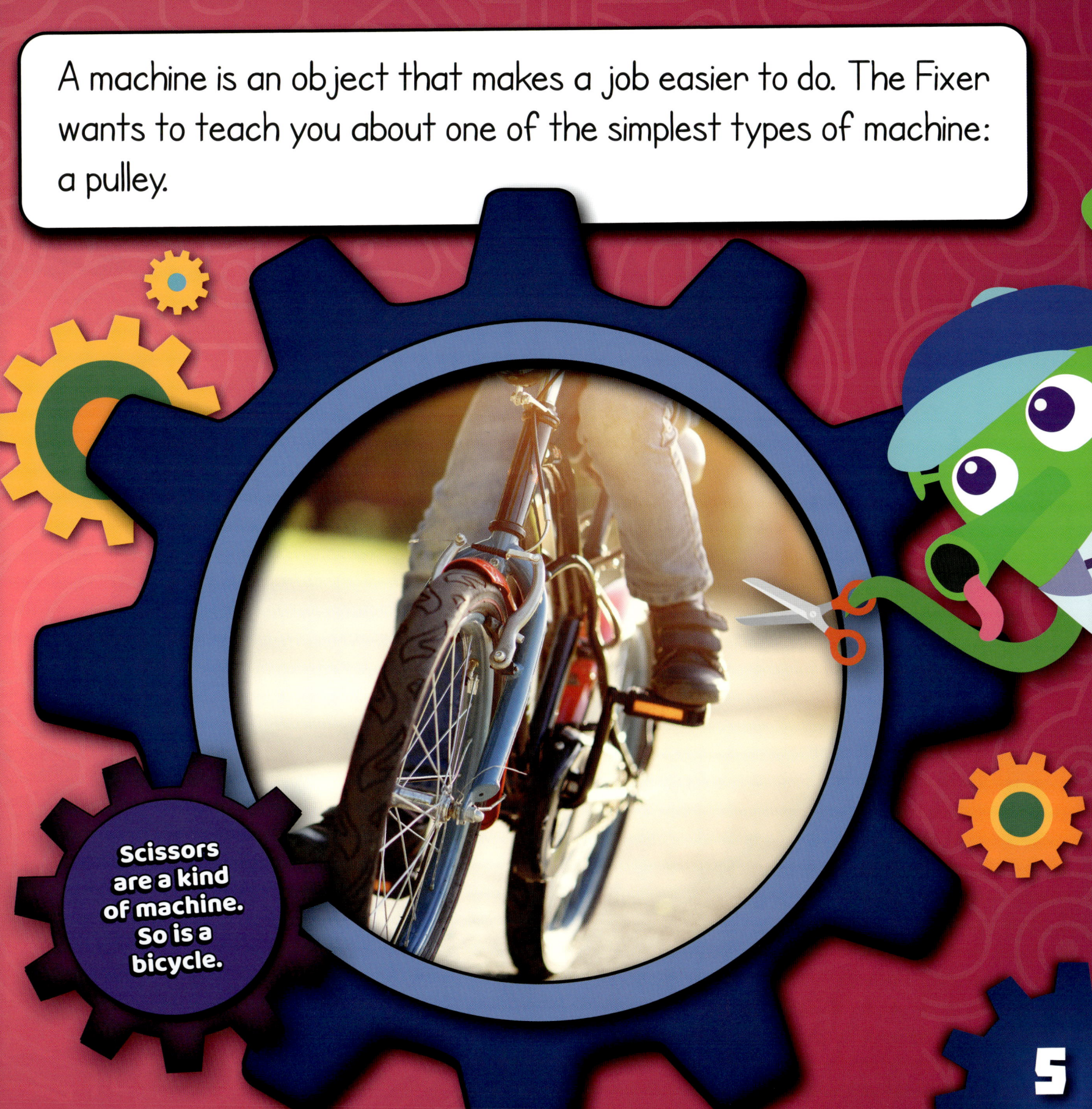

Scissors are a kind of machine. So is a bicycle.

PULLEYS

Pulleys are a type of simple machine that are used to lift heavy things. There are lots of different types of pulley <u>systems</u> for lots of different jobs. Each one looks a little bit different.

All pulleys have at least one wheel and a rope. The wheels of a pulley usually have <u>grooves</u> in them. This is so rope fits around them more easily.

Pulleys can use wire, string, chains or even steel cables instead of rope.

Steel cables

Here are some examples of pulleys.

Cranes use pulleys.

Pulleys are often found on boats and ships.

Pulleys are used to raise flags.

This bucket is lowered on a pulley.

Well

PFFFLUMLUMBMLUM!

The Fixer says that there may even be pulleys in your home. Here are a few.

Some clotheslines use pulleys.

Some garages use pulleys to open the doors.

Blinds use pulleys to move up and down.

PARTS OF A PULLEY

Pulley wheels with grooves, like this one, are called sheaves.

An axle is a small rod which goes through the middle of a wheel. The axle lets the wheel spin around. Sometimes the axle is fixed to the wheel, and sometimes the wheel spins freely around the axle.

Axle

The weight is the thing that you want to lift.

HOW A PULLEY WORKS

There is a part of a pulley that pulls one end of the rope. The other end of the rope is tied to an object. The heavier the object, the more <u>force</u> is needed to lift it.

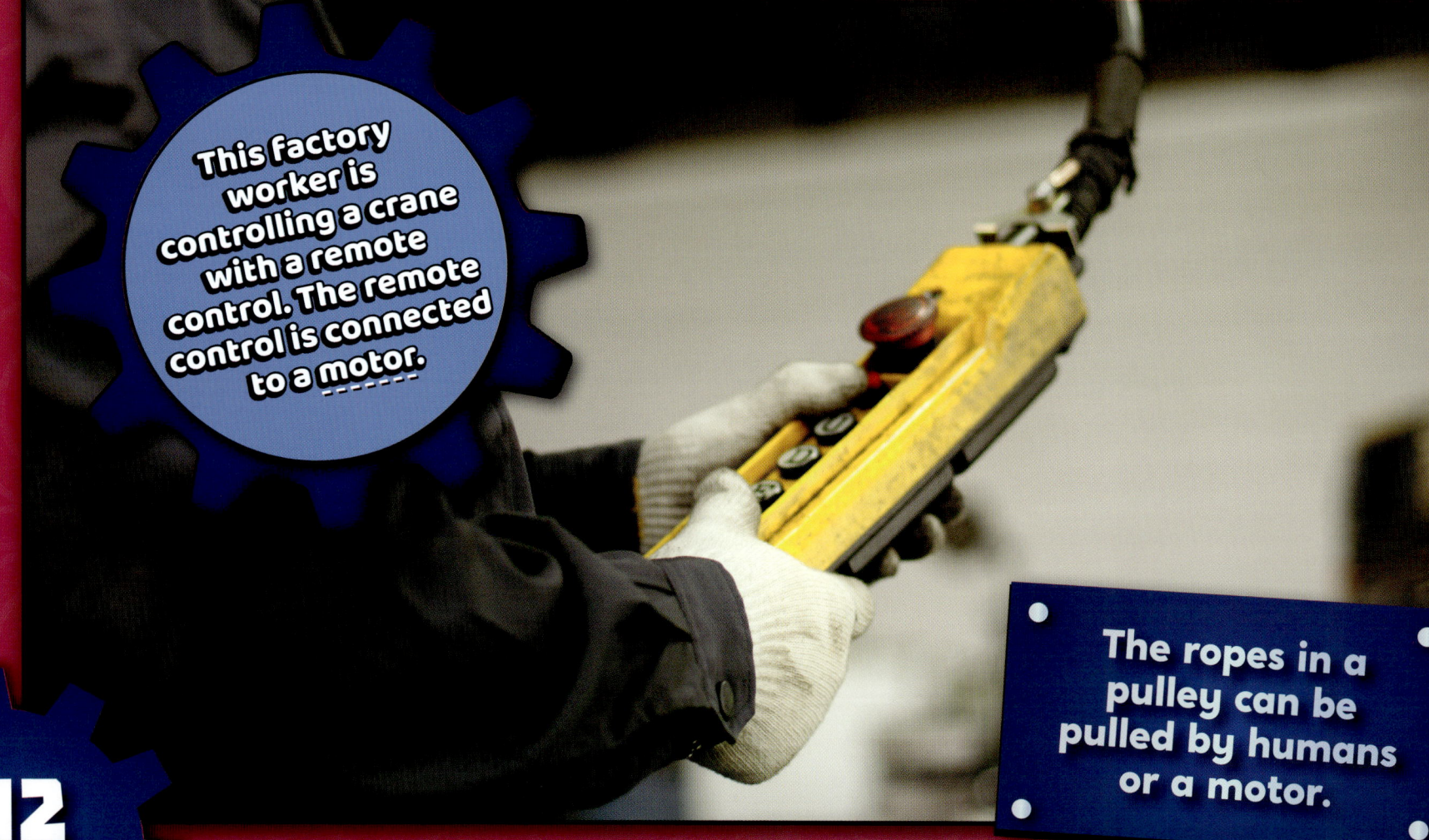

This factory worker is controlling a crane with a remote control. The remote control is connected to a <u>motor</u>.

The ropes in a pulley can be pulled by humans or a motor.

Friction is a force that happens when two things rub together. Friction slows things down and makes heat. There is friction between the rope and the pulley wheels.

You can feel the heat from friction when you rub your hands together quickly.

FLEEUGH!

It takes a little bit of extra force to overcome friction.

FIXED OR FREE?

Pulleys can either be fixed or free. In a fixed pulley, the wheel stays in the same place, and only the rope, wire or chain moves.

A flagpole is an example of a fixed pulley.

A free pulley is a wheel that moves along. A zipline is an example of a free pulley. The wheel moves along the wire.

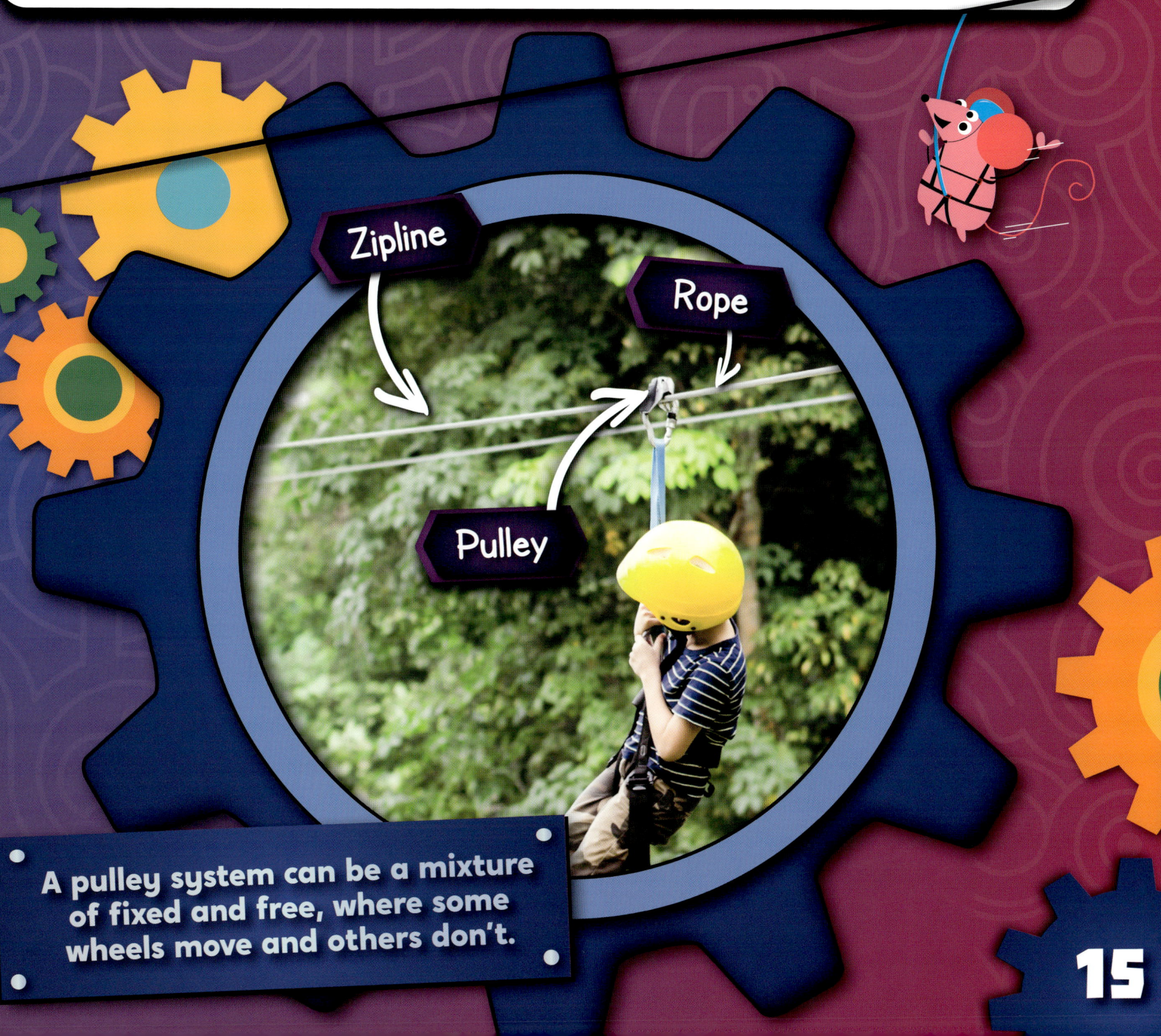

Zipline

Rope

Pulley

A pulley system can be a mixture of fixed and free, where some wheels move and others don't.

MORE WHEELS, MORE POWER

When a pulley has more than one wheel, it becomes easier to lift the object. If a pulley has two wheels, it takes half the force to lift the object.

Pulleys help people lift objects that would be too heavy to lift on their own.

More wheels mean even less force is needed. This is because the weight is evenly spread over the different parts of the rope. This is much better than having all the weight in one place.

Four wheels will take a quarter of the force to lift the same object.

LET'S BUILD A TOY LIFT

It is time to build! We will be using a pulley to make a lift that moves up and down. Get an adult to help you use scissors and tie knots.

YOU WILL NEED:

- 1 tall, rectangular cardboard box
- 1 smaller, square cardboard box that will fit inside the rectangular box
- Scissors
- 1 long piece of string
- 1 straw or tube
- 1 small, thin stick
- 1 pencil
- A piece of cardboard
- Some colouring pencils

19

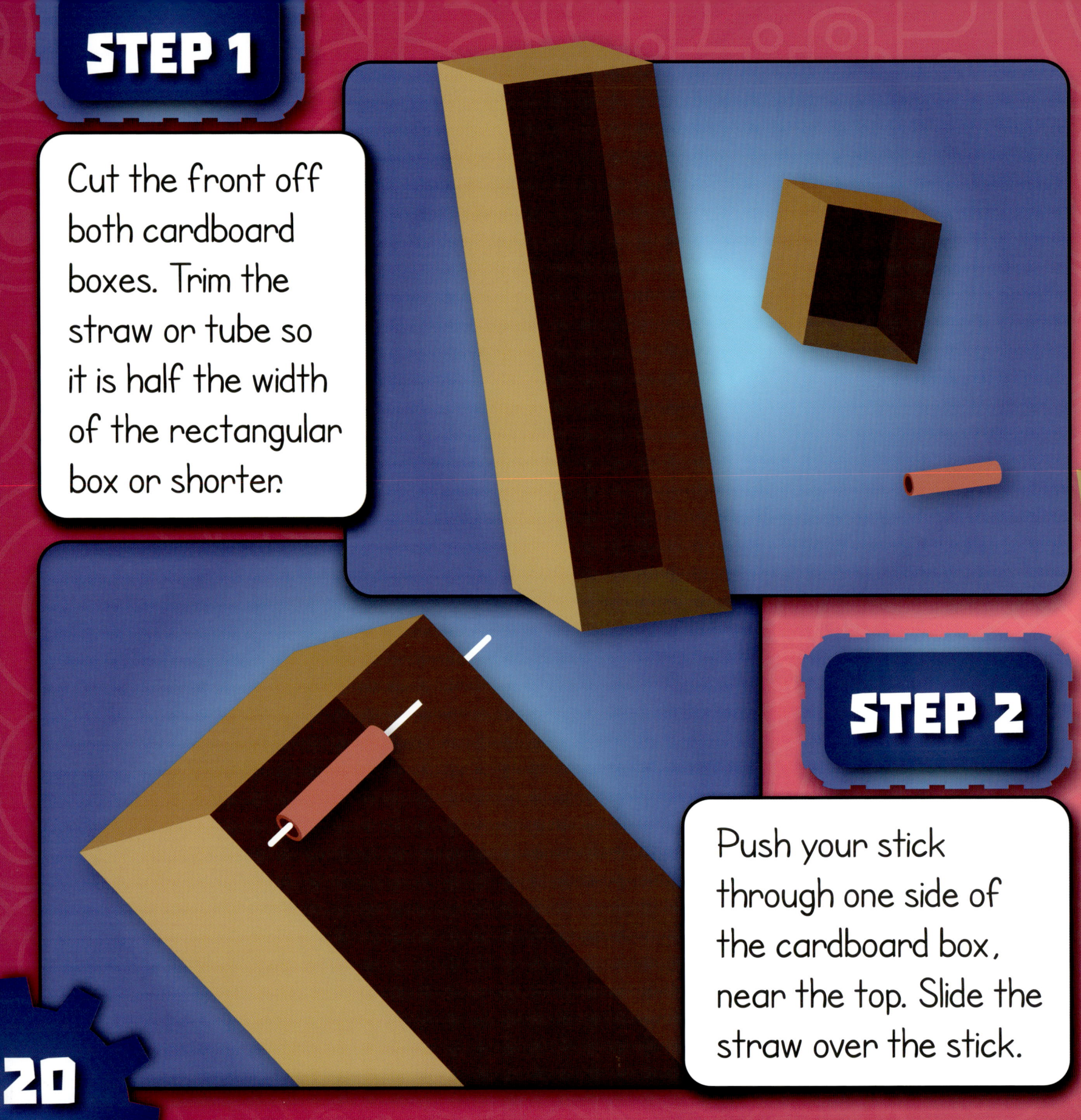

STEP 1

Cut the front off both cardboard boxes. Trim the straw or tube so it is half the width of the rectangular box or shorter.

STEP 2

Push your stick through one side of the cardboard box, near the top. Slide the straw over the stick.

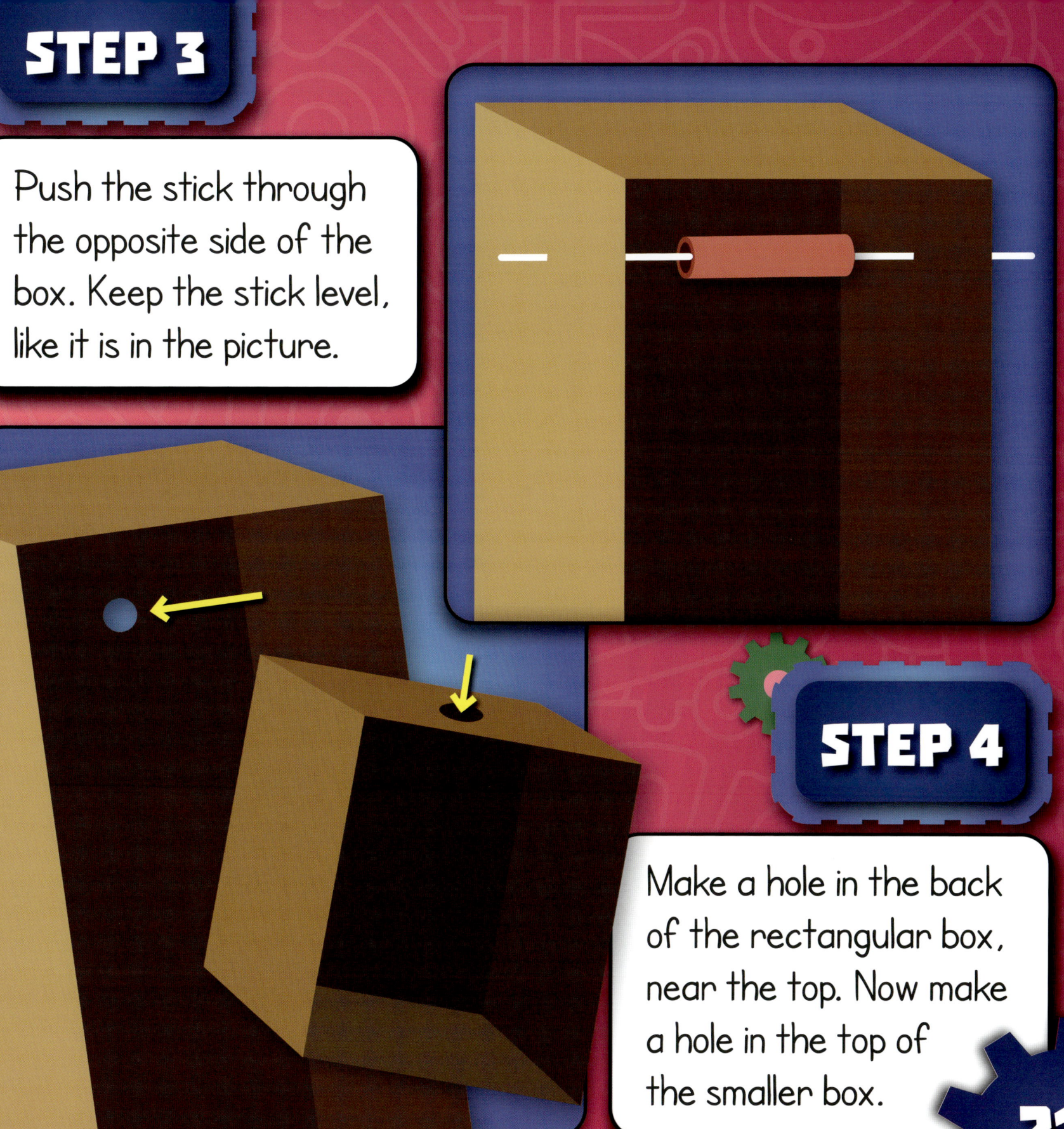

STEP 5

Push the string through the hole in the smaller box and tie a knot at the end.

STEP 6

Put the smaller box inside the rectangular box. Loop the other end of the string over the straw or tube and push it through the hole in the back of the rectangular box.

22

STEP 7

Use your pencils, scissors and piece of cardboard to make a character to go in your lift.

STEP 8

Put your character in the lift. Grab the end of the string behind the box and pull it downwards to see your lift go up!

GLOSSARY

force	a push or pull on an object
grooves	cuts or marks made in hard objects
motor	machines that make things move
overcome	to defeat, overpower or deal with something
systems	sets of things that work together to do specific jobs
universe	the space that everything exists in, including planets, galaxies and stars

INDEX

axles 10–11
cranes 8, 12
flags 8, 14
friction 13
grooves 7, 10
homes 9
machines 4–6
ropes 7, 10, 12–15, 17
spinning 11
weight 6, 10–12, 16–17
wheels 7, 10–11, 13–17